Thoughts on
SUCCESS

Thoughts on SUCCESS

TRIUMPH BOOKS
CHICAGO

Copyright © 1995 by FORBES INC. All rights reserved.

FORBES is a registered trademark of Forbes Inc.
The Forbes Leadership Library is a trademark of Forbes Inc.
Their use is pursuant to a license agreement with Forbes Inc.

This edition is published by Triumph Books, Chicago,
by arrangement with Forbes Inc.

Library of Congress Cataloging-in-Publication Data:
Thoughts on success.
    p. cm. — (The Forbes leadership library)
    Includes index.
    ISBN 1-57243-059-1
    1. Success—Quotations, maxims, etc. I. Forbes magazine.
II. Series.
PN6084.S78T46 1995
808.88'2—dc20   95-8052
                                            CIP

ISBN 1-57243-059-1 (paper)
ISBN 1-57243-075-3 (cloth)

This book is available in quantity at special discounts
for your group or organization. For more information, contact:

TRIUMPH BOOKS
644 S. Clark Street
Chicago, Illinois 60605
(312) 939-3330 FAX (312) 663-3557

Book design by Graffolio.
Cover design © 1995 by Triumph Books.
Illustrations from the Dover Pictorial Archive Series,
edited by Jim Harter (Dover Publications), used with permission.

Printed in the United States of America.

CONTENTS

INTRODUCTION

The moving motive in establishing FORBES Magazine, in 1917, was ardent desire to promulgate humaneness in business, then woefully lacking. . . .

Every issue of FORBES, since its inception, has appeared under the masthead: "With all thy getting, get understanding."

Not only so, but we have devoted, all through the years, a full page to "Thoughts on the Business of Life," reflections by ancient and modern sages calculated to inspire a philosophic mode of life, broad sympathies, charity towards all. . . .

I have faith that the time will eventually come when employees and employers, as well as all mankind, will realize that they serve themselves best when they serve others most.

B. C. Forbes

FOUNDATION STONES

In building a firm foundation for success, here are a few stones to remember:

The wisdom of preparation
The value of confidence
The worth of honesty
The privilege of working
The discipline of struggle
The magnetism of character
The radiance of health
The forcefulness of simplicity
The winsomeness of courtesy
The attractiveness of modesty
The inspiration of cleanliness
The satisfaction of serving
The power of suggestion
The buoyancy of enthusiasm
The advantage of initiative
The virtue of patience
The rewards of cooperation
The fruitfulness of perseverance
The sportsmanship of losing
The joy of winning

ROLLO C. HESTER

ACHIEVEMENT

Think of yourself as on the threshold
of unparalleled success.
A whole clear, glorious life lies before you.
Achieve! Achieve!

ANDREW CARNEGIE

Achievement is the death of endeavor
and the birth of disgust.

AMBROSE BIERCE

An uninspiring person believes
according to what he achieves.
An aspiring person achieves
according to what he believes.

SRI CHINMOY

Success is counted sweetest
by those who ne'er succeed.

EMILY DICKINSON

———— ·❈· ————

For unflagging interest and enjoyment,
a household of children,
if things go reasonably well,
certainly makes all other forms
of success and achievement
lose their importance by comparison.

THEODORE ROOSEVELT

———— ·❈· ————

So great has been the endurance,
so incredible the achievement, that,
as long as the sun
keeps a set course in heaven,
it would be foolish
to despair of the human race.

ERNEST L. WOODWARD

It takes a highly intellectual individual
to enjoy leisure. . . .
Most of us had better count on working.
What a man really wants
is creative challenge with sufficient skills
to bring him within the reach of success
so that he may have the expanding joy
of achievement.

DR. FAY B. NASH

Nothing splendid has ever been achieved
except by those who dared believe
that something inside them
was superior to circumstance.

BRUCE BARTON

Success is a ruthless competitor
for it flatters and nourishes our weaknesses
and lulls us into complacency.
We bask in the sunshine of accomplishment
and lose the spirit of humility
which helps us visualize all the factors
which have contributed to our success.

SAMUEL TILDEN

———✦———

Success is the reward for accomplishment.

HARRY F. BANKS

———✦———

The difference between failure and success
is doing a thing nearly right
and doing it exactly right.

EDWARD C. SIMMONS

The secret of the true love of work
is the hope of success in that work;
not for the money reward,
for the time spent, or for the skill exercised,
but for the successful result
in the accomplishment of the work itself.

SIDNEY A. WELTMER

You can't achieve anything
without getting in someone's way.
You can't be detached and effective.

ABBA EBAN

There are two things to aim at in life:
first to get what you want;
and after that, to enjoy it.
Only the wisest of mankind achieve the second.

LOGAN PEARSALL SMITH

ADVERSITY

A successful man is one who can lay
a firm foundation with the bricks
that others throw at him.

SIDNEY GREENBERG

Adversity makes men;
good fortune makes monsters.

FRENCH PROVERB

All adverse and depressing influences
can be overcome, not by fighting,
but by rising above them.

CHARLES CALEB COLTON

He that can heroically endure adversity
will bear prosperity with equal greatness of soul;
for the mind that cannot be dejected by the former
is not likely to be transported with the latter.

HENRY FIELDING

Don't be disquieted in time of adversity.
Be firm with dignity and self-reliant with vigor.

CHIANG KAI-SHEK

The superior man
makes the difficulty to be overcome his first interest;
success comes only later.

CONFUCIUS

The greatest obstacle to your success
is probably you.

FRANK TYGER

I have learned
that success is to be measured
not so much by the position
that one has reached in life
as by the obstacles
which he has overcome
while trying to succeed.

BOOKER T. WASHINGTON

If you succeed in life, you must do it
in spite of the efforts of others to pull you down.
There is nothing in the idea
that people are willing to help those
who help themselves. People are willing to help a man
who can't help himself,
but as soon as a man is able to help himself,
and does it, they join in making his life
as uncomfortable as possible.

EDGAR WATSON HOWE

In adversity assume the countenance of prosperity,
and in prosperity moderate the temper and desires.

LIVY

In prosperous times I have sometimes felt
my fancy and powers of language flag,
but adversity is to me
at least a tonic and bracer.

WALTER SCOTT

Most barriers to your success are man-made.
And most often, you're the man who made them.

FRANK TYGER

Let no one or anything stand
between you and the difficult task,
let nothing deny you this rich chance
to gain strength by adversity,
confidence by mastery, success by deserving it.
Do it better each time.
Do it better than anyone else can do it.

HARLOW H. CURTICE

Life affords no higher pleasure
than that of surmounting difficulties,
passing from one step of success to another,
forming new wishes and seeing them gratified.
He that labors in any great or laudable undertaking
has his fatigues first supported by hope
and afterwards rewarded by joy.

SAMUEL JOHNSON

One very important ingredient of success
is a good, wide-awake, persistent, tireless enemy.
An enemy to an ambitious man
is like the rhinoceros bird to the rhinoceros.
When the enemy comes,
the rhinoceros bird tells about it.
When a successful man is making mistakes,
the enemy immediately calls attention
and warns the man.
Get for yourself a first class enemy,
cultivate him as an enemy,
and when you achieve success, thank him.

COLONEL FRANK B. SHUTTS

Take care to be an economist in prosperity;
there is no fear of your being one in adversity.

JOHANN ZIMMERMAN

The friend of my adversity
I shall always cherish most.
I can better trust those who helped
to relieve the gloom of my dark hours
than those who are so ready to enjoy with me
the sunshine of my prosperity.

ULYSSES S. GRANT

Prosperity is too apt to prevent us
from examining our conduct;
but adversity leads us to think properly of our state,
and so is most beneficial to us.

SAMUEL JOHNSON

AMBITION

Ambition, confidence, enthusiasm, and success
are produced by courage, faith, pride and hard work.

HARRY F. BANKS

Ambition is an idol on whose wings
great minds are carried to extremes,
to be sublimely great, or to be nothing.

THOMAS SOUTHERN

Ambition is most aroused
by the trumpet clang of another's fame.

BALTASAR GRACIAN

Ambition is so powerful a passion
in the human breast
that however high we reach, we are never satisfied.

NICCOLÒ MACHIAVELLI

Every man has a secret ambition:
To outsmart horses, fish, and women.

MARK TWAIN

Most people would succeed in small things
if they were not troubled by great ambitions.

HENRY WADSWORTH LONGFELLOW

Ambition is the spur
that makes men struggle with destiny.
It is heaven's own incentive
to make purpose great and achievement greater.

DONALD G. MITCHELL

The desire not to be anything
is the desire not to be.

AYN RAND

Ambition is to the mind
what the cap is to the falcon;
it blinds us first, then compels us to tower
by reason of our blindness.

CHARLES CALEB COLTON

Ambition makes the same mistake
concerning power
that avarice makes as to wealth.
She begins by accumulating it
as a means to happiness, and finishes
by continuing to accumulate it
as an end.

CHARLES CALEB COLTON

Ambition is the germ from which
all growth of nobleness proceeds.

THOMAS D. ENGLISH

———

Every man is enthusiastic at times.
One man has enthusiasm for thirty minutes,
another man has it for thirty days,
but it is the man who has it for thirty years
who makes a success in life.

EDWARD B. BUTLER

———

Experience shows that success is due
less to ability than to zeal.
The winner is he who gives himself to his work,
body and soul.

CHARLES BUXTON

I found that the men and women
who got to the top
were those who did the jobs they had in hand,
with everything they had of energy
and enthusiasm and hard work.

HARRY S. TRUMAN

Many people have the ambition to succeed;
they may even have special aptitude for their job.
And yet they do not move ahead. Why?
Perhaps they think that since they can master
the job, there is no need to master themselves.

JOHN STEVENSON

The slave has but one master;
the man of ambition has as many as there are
people useful to his fortune.

JEAN DE LA BRUYÈRE

CHARACTER

A character standard is far more important
than even a gold standard.
The success of all economic systems
is still dependent upon both righteous leaders
and righteous people.
In the last analysis, our national future
depends upon our national character—
that is, whether it is spiritually or materially minded.

ROGER BABSON

A man's treatment of money
is the most decisive test of his character—
how he makes it and how he spends it.

JAMES MOFFATT

Character is the real foundation
of all worthwhile success.

JOHN HAYS HAMMOND

——————

You cannot build character and courage
by taking away man's initiative and independence.

ABRAHAM LINCOLN

——————

A quick and sound judgment,
good common sense, kind feeling,
and an instinctive perception of character,
in these are the elements of what is called tact,
which has so much to do
with acceptability and success in life.

CHARLES SIMMONS

A talent can be cultivated in tranquility;
a character only in the rushing stream of life.

JOHANN WOLFGANG VON GOETHE

Capitalism is the only system in the world
founded on credit and character.

HUBERT EATON

As diamonds cut diamonds,
and one hone smooths a second,
all the parts of intellect are whetstones to each other;
and genius, which is but the result
of their mutual sharpening, is character, too.

CYRUS A. BARTOL

It is sometimes frightening to observe the success
which comes even to the outlaw
with a polished technique . . .
But I believe we must reckon
with character in the end,
for it is as potent a force in world conflict
as it is in our own domestic affairs.
It strikes the last blow in any battle.

PHILIP D. REED

A man's true estate of power and riches
is to be in himself; not in his dwelling or position
or external relations,
but in his own essential character.

HENRY WARD BEECHER

Man is still responsible.
He must turn the alloy of modern experience
into the steel of mastery and character.
His success lies not with the stars but with himself.
He must carry on the fight
of self-correction and discipline.
He must fight mediocrity as sin
and live against the imperative
of life's highest ideal.

FRANK CURTIS WILLIAMS, D.D.

Our world is a college, events are teachers,
happiness is the graduating point,
character is the diploma God gives man.

NEWELL DWIGHT HILLIS

The most important thing for a young man is to
establish a credit—a reputation, character.

JOHN D. ROCKEFELLER

Moderate desires constitute a character
fitted to acquire all the good
which the world can yield.
He who has this character is prepared,
in whatever situation he is,
therewith to be content:
has learned the science of being happy;
and possesses the alchemic stone
which changes every metal into gold.

TIMOTHY DWIGHT

No legitimate business man
ever got started on the road to permanent success
by any other means than that of hard,
intelligent work,
coupled with an earned credit, plus character.

F. D. VAN AMBURGH

·- 27 -·

Our success in war and peace depends not on luck,
or rhetoric, or the intervention of mythical gods;
it depends on human character
and modern scientific creations,
and on respect for the meaning
and methods of science.

HARLOW SHAPLEY

———

The accumulation of property
is no guarantee of the development of character,
but the development of character,
or of any other good whatever,
is impossible without property.

WILLIAM GRAHAM SUMNER

CONFIDENCE

The first step in handling anything
is gaining the ability to face it.

L. RON HUBBARD

———

Confidence is that feeling by which the mind
embarks in great and honorable courses
with a sure hope and trust in itself.

CICERO

———

Confidence is the foundation
for all business relations.
The degree of confidence a man has in others,
and the degree of confidence others
have in him, determines a man's standing
in the commercial and industrial world.

WILLIAM J. H. BOETCKER

Skill and confidence
are an unconquered army.

GEORGE HERBERT

Each golden sunrise ushers in new opportunities
for those who retain faith in themselves,
and keep their chins up. No one has ever seen
a cock crow with its head down.
Courage to start and willingness to keep
everlastingly at it are the requisites for success.
Meet the sunrise with confidence.
Fill every golden minute with right thinking
and worthwhile endeavor.
Do this and there will be joy for you
in each golden sunset.

ALONZO NEWTON BENN

Blow your own horn loud.
If you succeed, people will forgive your noise;
if you fail, they'll forget it.

WILLIAM FEATHER

———

Faith in your own powers
and confidence in your individual methods
are essential to success.

RODERICK STEVENS

———

Fight! Be somebody! If you have lost confidence
in yourself, make believe you are somebody else,
somebody that's got brains, and act like him.

SOL HESS

———

If at first you do succeed,
it can give you a false sense of importance.

FRANK TYGER

I invest in yourself—
if you have confidence in yourself.

WILLIAM FEATHER

Man must be arched and buttressed from within,
else the temple will crumble to dust.

MARCUS AURELIUS ANTONINUS

Success in business implies optimism,
mutual confidence, and fair play.
A business man must hold a high opinion
of the worth of what he has to sell,
and he must feel that he
is a useful public servant.

R. H. CABELL

The percentage of mistakes in quick decisions
is no greater than in long-drawn-out vacillations,
and the effect of decisiveness itself
"makes things go" and creates confidence.

ANNE O'HARE MCCORMICK

The pious and just honoring of ourselves
may be thought the fountainhead from whence
every laudable and worthy enterprise issues forth.

JOHN MILTON

This country was not built by men who relied
on somebody else to take care of them.
It was built by men who relied on themselves,
who dared to shape their own lives,
who had enough courage to blaze new trails—
enough confidence in themselves
to take the necessary risks.

J. OLLIE EDMUNDS

COURAGE

Courage conquers all things.

OVID

Courage is what it takes
to stand up and speak;
courage is also what it takes
to sit down and listen.

WINSTON S. CHURCHILL

Courage, it would seem, is nothing less
than the power to overcome danger,
misfortune, fear, injustice, while continuing
to affirm inwardly that life
with all its sorrows is good;
that everything is meaningful even if
in a sense beyond our understanding;
and that there is always tomorrow.

DOROTHY THOMPSON

Courage leads starward,
fear toward death.

SENECA

Courage is grace under pressure.

ERNEST HEMINGWAY

Success is never final and failure never fatal.
It's courage that counts.

GEORGE F. TILTON

Courage is worth nothing
if the gods withhold their aid.

EURIPIDES

Courage consists in equality
to the problem before us.

RALPH WALDO EMERSON

Courage is a virtue only so far as
it is directed to produce.

FRANÇOIS FÉNELON

Courage and perseverance
have a magical talisman,
before which difficulties disappear
and obstacles vanish into air.

JOHN QUINCY ADAMS

Don't be afraid to take a big step
if one is indicated.
You can't cross a chasm
in two small jumps.

DAVID LLOYD GEORGE

Set the course of your lives
by the three stars—
sincerity, courage, unselfishness.
From these flow a host of other virtues. . . .
He who follows them
and does not seek success,
will attain the highest type of success,
that which lies in the esteem of those
among whom he dwells.

DR. MONROE E. DEUTSCH

Failure is only postponed success
as long as courage "coaches" ambition.
The habit of persistence
is the habit of victory.

HERBERT KAUFMAN

Fix your eyes upon the greatness of your country
as you have it before you day by day . . .
and when you feel her great,
remember that her greatness
was won by men with courage,
with knowledge of their duty
and with a sense of honor in action,
who, even if they failed in some venture,
would not think of depriving
their country of their powers
but laid them at her feet as their fairest offering.

PERICLES

It is courage the world needs,
not infallibility . . .
courage is always the surest wisdom.

WILFRED T. GRENFELL

The difference between getting
somewhere and nowhere
is the courage to make an early start.
The fellow who sits still
and does just what he is told
will never be told to do big things.

CHARLES M. SCHWAB

The greatest asset of any nation
is the spirit of its people,
and the greatest danger
that can menace any nation
is the breakdown of that spirit—
the will to win and the courage to work.

GEORGE B. COURTELYOU

The only security is courage.

FRANÇOIS DE LA ROCHEFOUCAULD

The strongest, most generous
and proudest
of all virtues is courage.

MICHEL DE MONTAIGNE

Success is the child of audacity.

BENJAMIN DISRAELI

DESTINY

Blaming destiny is a poor out
for those who don't reach
desired destinations.

MALCOLM S. FORBES

Character is destiny.

HERACLITUS

Ideals are like stars:
you will not succeed in touching them
with your hands, but like the seafaring man
on the desert of waters, you choose them
as your guides, and following them,
you reach your destiny.

CARL SCHURZ

Success is a journey—
not a destination.

H. TOM COLLARD

Let us follow our destiny, ebb and flow.
Whatever may happen,
we master fortune by accepting it.

VIRGIL

Men are born to succeed—
not to fail.

HENRY DAVID THOREAU

Misfortune does not always wait on vice;
nor is success the constant guest of virtue.

WILLIAM HAVARD

To find a career to which you are
adapted by nature,
and then to work hard at it,
is about as near to a formula
for success and happiness
as the world provides.
One of the fortunate aspects
of this formula is that,
granted the right career has been found,
the hard work takes care of itself.
Then hard work is not hard work at all.

MARK SULLIVAN

———————

We do not know, in most cases,
how far social failure and success
are due to heredity,
and how far to environment.
But environment is the easier
of the two to improve.

J. B. S. HALDANE

My destiny is solitude,
and my life is work.

RICHARD WAGNER

The cause of freedom is identified
with the destinies of humanity,
and in whatever part of the world
it gains ground by and by,
it will be a common gain
to all those who desire it.

LOUIS KOSSUTH

The road to success
is usually off the beaten path.

FRANK TYGER

We sow our thoughts, and we reap our actions;
we sow our actions, and we reap our habits;
we sow our habits and we reap our characters;
we sow our characters and we reap our destiny.

CHARLES A. HALL

DETERMINATION

All the world over it is true
that a double-minded man
is unstable in all his ways,
like a wave on the streamlet,
tossed hither and thither
with every eddy of its tide.
A determinate purpose in life
and a steady adhesion to it
through all disadvantages,
are indispensable conditions of success.

WILLIAM M. PUNSHON

Decision and determination
are the engineer and fireman of our train
to opportunity and success.

BURT LAWLOR

Either attempt it not, or succeed.

OVID

If you would succeed in life,
it is of first importance
that your individuality,
your independence,
your determination be trained
that you not be lost in the crowd.

ORISON SWETT MARDEN

This world is given as the prize
for the men in earnest.

FREDERICK W. ROBERTSON

Success seems to be largely a matter of
hanging on after others have let go.

WILLIAM FEATHER

The successful man lengthens his stride
when he discovers that the signpost has deceived him;
the failure looks for a place to sit down.

J. R. ROGERS

———◆———

There hath grown no grass on my heels
since I went hence.

NICHOLAS UDALL

———◆———

Success in business
does not depend upon genius.
Any young man of ordinary intelligence
who is normally sound and not afraid to work
should succeed in spite of obstacles and handicaps
if he plays the game fairly
and keeps everlastingly at it.

JAMES C. PENNEY

Nothing, not even sheer ability,
can make up for the dedication required
for a successful business career.

RAY EPPERT

There is nothing in the world really beneficial
that does not lie within the reach
of an informed understanding
and a well-protected pursuit.

EDMUND BURKE

We do not meet with success
except by reiterated efforts.

FRANÇOISE DE MAINTENON

When business is not all that it should be,
there is a temptation to sit back and say,
"Well, what's the use!
We've done everything possible
to stir up a little business
and there is nothing doing
so what's the use of trying!"
There is always a way. There was a way in,
and there is a way out.
And success comes to the man
who grits his teeth, squares his jaw, and says,
"There is a way for me and, by jingo, I'll find it."
The stagnator gathers green scum,
finally dries up and leaves an unsightly hollow.

CLIFFORD SLOAN

You do not succeed because
you do not know what you want,
or you don't want it intensely enough.

FRANK CRANE

DREAMS

Hold fast to dreams, for if dreams die, life is a
broken-winged bird that cannot fly.

LANGSTON HUGHES

Always dream and shoot higher
than you know you can do.
Don't bother just to be better
than your contemporaries or predecessors.
Try to be better than yourself.

WILLIAM FAULKNER

Keep your eyes on the stars
and your feet on the ground.

THEODORE ROOSEVELT

The very substance of the ambitious
is merely the shadow of a dream.

WILLIAM SHAKESPEARE

Dreamers and doers—
the world generally divides men
into those two general classifications,
but the world is often wrong.
There are men who win the admiration
and respect of their fellowmen.
They are the men worth while.
Dreaming is just another name
for thinking, planning, devising—
another way of saying
that a man exercises his soul.
A steadfast soul,
holding steadily to a dream ideal,
plus a sturdy will
determined to succeed in any venture,
can make any dream come true.
Use your mind and your will.
They work together for you beautifully
if you'll only give them a chance.

B. N. MILLS

Dreams never hurt anybody
if he keeps working right behind the dream
to make as much of it come real as he can.

FRANK W. WOOLWORTH

Happiness should always remain
a bit incomplete.
After all, dreams are boundless.

ANATOLY KARPOV

Happy are those who dream dreams
and are ready to pay the price
to make them come true.

LEON J. SUENENS

The life of a man consists not in seeing visions
and in dreaming dreams, but in active charity
and in willing service.

HENRY WADSWORTH LONGFELLOW

Imagination is the secret reservoir
of the riches of the human race.

MAUDE L. FRANDSEN

If one advances confidently
in the direction of his dreams,
and endeavors to live the life
which he has imagined,
he will meet with a success
unexpected in common hours.

HENRY DAVID THOREAU

I hope the day will never come
when the American nation
will be the champion of the status quo.
Once that happens, we shall have forfeited,
and rightly forfeited,
the support of the unsatisfied,
of those who are the victims
of inevitable imperfections,
of those who, young in years or spirit,
believe that they can make a better world
and of those who dream dreams
and want to make their dreams come true.

JOHN FOSTER DULLES

———

Ideas must work
through the brains and the arms
of good and brave men,
or they are no better than dreams.

RALPH WALDO EMERSON

Some men see things as they are
and ask, "Why?"
I dream things that never were
and ask, "Why not?"

ROBERT F. KENNEDY

There is no shame in having fallen.
Nor any shame in being born
into a lowly estate.
There is only shame
in not struggling to rise.
And also shame
for not wishing to attain the better.
Or not dreaming about it
and praying for it.

SAMUEL AMALU

We sometimes from dreams
pick up some hint
worth improving by . . . reflection.

THOMAS JEFFERSON

Your imagination has much to do with your life.
It pictures beauty, success, desired results.
On the other hand, it brings into focus ugliness,
distress, and failure. It is for you to decide
how you want your imagination to serve you.

PHILIP CONLEY

FAILURE

Be awful nice to 'em goin' up,
because you're gonna meet 'em all comin' down.

JIMMY DURANTE

Generally speaking,
success brings out the actors' worst qualities
and failure the best.

GEORGE ABBOTT

If I die prematurely,
at any rate I shall be saved from being bored
by my own success.

SAMUEL BUTLER

To be successful,
you've got to be willing to fail.

FRANK TYGER

The secret of success in life
is known only to those
who have not succeeded.

J. CHURTON COLLINS

Nobody succeeds in a big way
except by risking failure.

WILLIAM FEATHER

Shirking easily becomes a habit
as difficult to throw off
as the use of drugs
and has ruined many men's
chances for success.

HENRY L. DOHERTY

If I wanted to become a tramp,
I would seek information and advice
from the most successful tramp I could find.
If I wanted to become a failure
I would seek advice from men
who have never succeeded.
If I wanted to succeed in all things,
I would look around me
for those who are succeeding,
and do as they have done.

JOSEPH MARSHALL WADE

Sometimes a noble failure
serves the world as faithfully
as a distinguished success.

EDWARD DOWDEN

Success comes to those
who become success conscious.
Failure comes to those
who indifferently allow themselves
to become failure conscious.

NAPOLEON HILL

Success has ruin'd many a man.

BENJAMIN FRANKLIN

Success is the brand on the brow
of the man who has aimed too low.

JOHN MASEFIELD

The ladder of life is full of splinters,
but they always prick the hardest
when we're sliding down.

WILLIAM L. BROWNELL

The line between failure and success is so fine
that we scarcely know when we pass it—
so fine that we often are on the line
and do not know it.

RALPH WALDO EMERSON

The secret of success
of every man who has ever been successful
lies in the fact that he formed the habit
of doing those things
failures don't like to do.

A. JACKSON KING

There isn't much thrill in success
unless one has first been close to failure.

WILLIAM FEATHER

———

To be ambitious for wealth,
and yet always expecting to be poor;
to be always doubting your ability
to get what you long for,
is like trying to reach east by traveling west.
There is no philosophy
which will help man to succeed
when he is always doubting his ability to do so,
and thus attracting failure.
No matter how hard you work for success,
if your thought is saturated
with the fear of failure,
it will kill your efforts,
neutralize your endeavors
and make success impossible.

CHARLES BAUDOUIN

We mount to heaven
mostly on the ruins
of our cherished schemes,
finding our failures were successes.

AMOS BRONSON ALCOTT

You and I must not complain
if our plans break down
if we have done our part.
That probably means that the plans
of One who knows more than we do
have succeeded.

EDWARD E. HALE

FRIENDSHIP

A friendship founded on business
is a good deal better
than a business founded on friendship.

JOHN D. ROCKEFELLER

━━◆◆◆━━

A true friend never gets in your way
unless you happen to be going down.

ARNOLD GLASOW

━━◆◆◆━━

Every man, however wise,
needs the advice of
some sagacious friend
in the affairs of life.

PLAUTUS

━━◆◆◆━━

Few men have the natural strength
to honor a friend's success without envy.

AESCHYLUS

Friends are an aid to the young,
to guard them from error;
to the elderly, to attend to their wants
and to supplement their failing power of action;
to those in the prime of life,
to assist them to noble deeds.

ARISTOTLE

Friendship
is a strong and habitual inclination in two persons
to promote the good and happiness
of one another.

EUSTACE BUDGELL

Friendship is the only cement
that will ever hold the world together.

WOODROW WILSON

He is our friend
who loves more than admires us,
and would aid us in our great work.

WILLIAM ELLERY CHANNING

If you have no friends
to share or rejoice in your success in life—
if you cannot look back to those
to whom you owe gratitude,
or forward to those to whom
you ought to afford protection,
still it is no less incumbent on you
to move steadily in the path of duty;
for your active exertions
are due not only to society;
but in humble gratitude
to the Being who made you a member of it,
with powers to serve yourself and others.

WALTER SCOTT

If you'll forget the things you give
And ne'er forget what you receive;
Quite soon you'll make a host of friends
Who'll gladly aid you to achieve.

ALONZO NEWTON BENN

It is a good thing to be rich,
it is a good thing to be strong,
but it is a better thing
to be beloved of many friends.

EURIPIDES

Real success is not on the stage,
but off the stage is a human being,
and how you get along
with your fellow men.

SAMMY DAVIS, JR.

The ability to form friendships,
to make people believe in you and trust you,
is one of the few
absolutely fundamental qualities of success.
Selling, buying, negotiating
are so much smoother and easier
when the parties enjoy each other's confidence.
The young man who can make friends quickly
will find that he will glide
instead of stumbling through life.

JOHN J. MCGUIRK

The making of friends who are real friends
is the best token we have
of a man's success in life.

EDWARD E. HALE

The man or woman
who treasures his friends
is usually solid gold himself.

MARJORIE HOLMES

The most important single ingredient
in the formula of success
is knowing how to get along with people.

THEODORE ROOSEVELT

We are all travelers
in the desert of life
and the best we can find in our journey
is an honest friend.

ROBERT LOUIS STEVENSON

What are friends for if you don't use them?

FREDDIE MYERS

Years and years of happiness
only make us realize how lucky we are
to have friends that have shared
and made that happiness a reality.

ROBERT E. FREDERICK

When fortune smiles, what need of friends?

EURIPIDES

HAPPINESS

No one's happiness but my own
is in my power to achieve or to destroy.

AYN RAND

Happiness and misery depend not
upon how high up or low down you are—
they depend not upon these,
but on the direction in which you are tending.

SAMUEL BUTLER

Happiness consists more in small conveniences
or pleasures that occur every day,
than in great pieces of good fortune
that happen but seldom to a man
in the course of his life.

BENJAMIN FRANKLIN

It is not in doing what you like,
but in liking what you do
that is the secret of happiness.

JAMES M. BARRIE

Happiness is a dividend
on a well-invested life.

DUNCAN STUART

I look on that man as happy who,
when there is a question of success,
looks into his work for a reply.

RALPH WALDO EMERSON

Happiness is only a by-product
of successful living.

DR. AUSTEN FOX RIGGS

Here below is not the land of happiness;
it is only the land of toil;
and every joy which comes to us
is only to strengthen us
for some greater labor that is to succeed.

IMMANUEL FICHTE

———

I believe in the possibility of happiness,
if one cultivates intuition
and outlives the grosser passions,
including optimism.

GEORGE SANTAYANA

If you observe a really happy man,
you will find him building a boat,
writing a symphony,
educating his son,
growing double dahlias,
or looking for dinosaur eggs in the Gobi Desert.
He will not be searching for happiness
as if it were a collar button
that had rolled under the radiator,
striving for it as the goal itself.
He will have become aware
that he is happy in the course of living life
twenty-four crowded hours of each day.

W. BERAN WOLFE

Planning for happiness
is rarely successful.
Happiness just happens.

ROBERT HALF

If virtue promises
happiness, prosperity and peace,
then progress in virtue
is progress in each of these;
for to whatever point
the perfection of anything brings us,
progress is always an approach toward it.

EPICTETUS

Mankind differ
in their notions of happiness;
but in my opinion he truly possesses it
who lives in the anticipation of honest fame,
and the glorious figure he shall make
in the eyes of posterity.

PLINY THE YOUNGER

Money never made a man happy yet,
nor will it.
There is nothing in its nature
to produce happiness.

BENJAMIN FRANKLIN

Search for a single, inclusive good
is doomed to failure.
Such happiness as life is capable of
comes from the full participation of all our powers
in the endeavor to wrest
from each changing situation of experience
its own full and unique meaning.

JOHN DEWEY

Someone has well said,
"Success is a journey, not a destination."
Happiness is to be found along the way,
not at the end of the road.

ROBERT R. UPDEGRAFF

Success is getting what you want,
happiness is wanting what you get.

DAVE GARDNER

The hours we pass
with happy prospects in view
are more pleasing than those
crowded with fruition.

OLIVER GOLDSMITH

The road to happiness lies
in two simple principles:
find what it is that interests you
and that you can do well,
and when you find it
put your whole soul into it—
every bit of energy and ambition
and natural ability you have.

JOHN D. ROCKEFELLER

We rich men count our happiness to lie
in the little superfluities, not in necessities.

PLUTARCH

We never enjoy perfect happiness;
our most fortunate successes
are mingled with sadness;
some anxieties always perplex
the reality of our satisfaction.

PIERRE CORNEILLE

What a man does with his wealth
depends upon his idea of happiness.
Those who draw prizes in life
are apt to spend tastelessly, if not viciously,
not knowing that it requires as much talent
to spend as to make.

EDWIN P. WHIPPLE

What is happiness?—
The feeling that power increases—
that resistance is overcome.

FRIEDRICH W. NIETZSCHE

The secret of success in society
is a certain heartiness and sympathy.
A man who is not happy in company,
cannot find any word in his memory
that will fit the occasion;
all his information is a little impertinent.
A man who is happy there,
finds in every turn of the conversation
occasions for the introduction of what he has to say.
The favorites of society are able men,
and of more spirit than wit,
who have no uncomfortable egotism,
but who exactly fill the hour and the company,
contended and contenting.

RALPH WALDO EMERSON

Where ambition ends,
happiness begins.

HUNGARIAN PROVERB

You never see the stock called Happiness
quoted on the exchange.

HENRY VAN DYKE

INITIATIVE

Details often kill initiative,
but there have been few successful men
who weren't good at details.
Don't ignore details. Lick them.

WILLIAM B. GIVEN, JR.

Genius is initiative on fire.

HOLBROOK JACKSON

I can give you a six-word formula
for success:
"Think things through—
then follow through."

EDWARD RICKENBACKER

I will spit on my hands
and take better hold.

JOHN HEYWOOD

Success is often just an idea away.

FRANK TYGER

If you want to succeed,
you should strike out on new paths
rather than travel the worn paths
of accepted success.

JOHN D. ROCKEFELLER

Initiative is to success
what a lighted match is to a candle.

ORLANDO A. BATTISTA

To get anywhere,
strike out for somewhere,
or you'll get nowhere.

MARTHA LUPTON

Our vast progress in transportation,
past and future, is only a symbol
of the progress that is possible
by constantly striving toward new horizons
in every human activity.
Who can say what new horizons lie before us
if we can but maintain the initiative
and develop the imagination to penetrate them—
new economic horizons,
new horizons in the art of government,
new social horizons,
new horizons expanding in all directions,
to the end that greater degrees of well-being
may be enjoyed by everyone, everywhere.

ALFRED P. SLOAN, JR.

Success won't just come to you.
It has to be met at least halfway.

FRANK TYGER

It is the direct man
who strikes sledgehammer blows,
who penetrates the very marrow of a subject
at every stroke
and gets the meat out of a proposition,
who does things.

ORISON SWETT MARDEN

The key to whatever success I enjoy today is:
Don't ask.
Do.

VIKKI CARR

The men who try to do something and fail
are infinitely better than those
who try nothing and succeed.

LLOYD JONES

INTEGRITY

A great business success
was probably never attained by chasing the dollar,
but is due to pride in one's work—
the pride that makes business an art.

HENRY L. DOHERTY

A little integrity is better than any career.

RALPH WALDO EMERSON

A successful life is not an easy life.
It is built upon strong qualities, sacrifice,
endeavor, loyalty, integrity.

GRANT D. BRANDON

Success can corrupt;
usefulness can only exalt.

DIMITRI MITROPOLOUS

Every man should make up his mind
that if he expects to succeed, he must give
an honest return for the other man's dollar.

EDWARD H. HARRIMAN

I do the very best I know how—
the very best I can;
and mean to keep doing so until the end.
If the end brings me out all right,
what is said against me
won't amount to anything.
If the end brings me out wrong,
ten angels swearing I was right
would make no difference.

ABRAHAM LINCOLN

For employee success,
loyalty and integrity
are equally as important as ability.

HARRY F. BANKS

If a man successful in business
expends a part of his income
in things of no real use,
while the poor employed by him
pass through difficulties
in getting the necessaries of life,
this requires his serious attention.

JOHN WOOLMAN

Integrity is the first step to true greatness.
Men love to praise,
but are slow to practice it.

CHARLES SIMMONS

Man cannot be satisfied with mere success.
He is concerned with the terms
upon which success comes to him.
And very often the terms seem
more important than the success.

CHARLES A. BENNETT

Mark, young man, the line you succeed in
will be of your own finding.
The Davids in life do not slay the Goliaths
of difficulty and temptation
in another's armor, even though it be the king's,
but with their own self-made weapons,
though they be nothing more formidable
than a sling and a pebble.

G. E. BISHOP

Our definition of success is unorthodox.
We claim that any man who is honest, fair, tolerant,
kindly, charitable of others and well behaved
is a success, no matter what his station in life.

JAY E. HOUSE

The man who will use his skill
and constructive imagination
to see how much he can give for a dollar,
instead of how little he can give for a dollar,
is bound to succeed.

HENRY FORD

The private and personal blessings we enjoy,
the blessings of immunity, safeguard, liberty,
and integrity, deserve the thanksgiving of a whole life.

JEREMY TAYLOR

The vital force in business life
is the honest desire to serve.
Business, it is said,
is the science of service.
He profits most who serves best.
At the very bottom
of the wish to render service
must be honesty of purpose,
and, as I go along through life,
I see more and more
that honesty in word, thought, and work
means success.
It spells a life worth living
and in business clean success.

GEORGE EBERHARD

You, yourself, have got to see
that there is no just interpretation of life
except in terms of life's best things.
No pleasure philosophy, no sensuality,
no place nor power, no material success
can for a moment give such inner satisfaction
as the sense of living for good purposes,
for maintenance of integrity,
for the preservation of self-approval.

MINOT SIMONS

OPPORTUNITY

Every successful man I have heard of
has done the best he could
with conditions as he found them,
and not waited until the next year for better.

EDGAR WATSON HOWE

Opportunity is the best captain of all endeavor.

SOPHOCLES

The great secret of success in life
is for a man to be ready
when his opportunity comes.

BENJAMIN DISRAELI

Next to knowing when to seize an opportunity,
the most important thing in life
is to know when to forego an advantage.

BENJAMIN DISRAELI

I do not want anybody to convince my son
that some one will guarantee him a living.
I want him rather to realize
that there is plenty of opportunity
in this country for him to achieve success,
but whether he wins or loses
depends entirely on his own character,
perseverance, thrift, intelligence,
and capacity for hard work.

MAJOR JOHN L. GRIFFITH

No great man ever complains
of want of opportunity.

RALPH WALDO EMERSON

No man can make his opportunity.
He can only make use of such opportunities as occur.

FORREST P. SHERMAN

Nobody's problem is ideal.
Nobody has things just as he would like them.
The thing to do is to make a success
with what material I have.
It is sheer waste of time and soul-power
to imagine what I would do if things were different.
They are not different.

DR. FRANK CRANE

The ladder of success doesn't care who climbs it.

FRANK TYGER

One big reason why men do not develop greater
abilities, greater sales strength, greater resourcefulness
is because they use neither their abilities
nor their opportunities.
We don't need more strength or more ability
or greater opportunity.
What we need is to use what we have.
Men fail and their families suffer deprivations
when all the time these men have
in their possession the same assets other men
are utilizing to accumulate a fortune. . . .
Life doesn't cheat. It doesn't pay in counterfeit coin.
It doesn't lock up shop and go home
when payday comes.
It pays every man exactly what he has earned.
The age-old law that a man gets what he earns
hasn't been suspended.
When we take that truth home and believe it,
we've turned a big corner on the high road
that runs straight through to success.

BASIL S. WALSH

The man who works
need never be a problem to anyone.
Opportunities multiply as they are seized;
they die when neglected.
Life is a long line of opportunities.

JOHN WICKER

———————

The most successful business man
is the man who holds onto the old
just as long as it is good
and grabs the new just as soon as it is better.

ROBERT P. VANDERPOEL

———————

There is a tide in the affairs of men, which,
taken at the flood, leads on to fortune;
omitted, all the voyage of their life is bound
in shallows and in miseries.

WILLIAM SHAKESPEARE

There is no security on this earth.
Only opportunity.

DOUGLAS MACARTHUR

———

True success is the only thing that you cannot have
unless and until you have offered it to others.

SRI CHINMOY

———

Vigilance in watching opportunity;
tact and daring in seizing upon opportunity;
force and persistence in crowding opportunity
to its utmost possible achievement—
these are the martial virtues
which must command success.

AUSTIN PHELPS

What is opportunity
to the man who can't use it?
An unfecundated egg,
which the waves of time
wash away into nonentity.

GEORGE ELIOT

(MARY ANN EVANS)

PATIENCE

A handful of patience
is worth more than a bushel of brains.

DUTCH PROVERB

A leaf that is destined to grow large
is full of grooves and wrinkles at the start.
Now if one has no patience
and wants it smooth offhand like a willow leaf,
there is trouble ahead.

JOHANN WOLFGANG VON GOETHE

All human power
is a compound of time and patience.

HONORÉ DE BALZAC

Genius is patience.

GEORGE-LOUIS LECLERC DE BUFFON

Have patience with all things,
but chiefly have patience with yourself.
Do not lose courage
in considering your own imperfections,
but instantly start remedying them—
every day begin the task anew.

ST. FRANCIS DE SALES

He that has no patience
has nothing at all.

ITALIAN PROVERB

In most things success depends on
knowing how long it takes to succeed.

MONTESQUIEU

(CHARLES-LOUIS DE SECONDAT)

It is natural to every man to wish for distinction;
and the praise of those who can confer honor
by their praise, in spite of all false philosophy,
is sweet to every human heart;
but as eminence can be but the lot of a few,
patience of obscurity
is a duty which we owe
not more to our own happiness
than to the quiet of the world at large.

SYDNEY SMITH

It is not necessary for all great men
to be great in action.
The greatest and most sublime power
is often simple patience.

HORACE BUSHNELL

On the whole, it is patience
which makes the final difference
between those who succeed
or fail in all things.
All the greatest people
have it in an infinite degree,
and among the less, the patient weak ones
always conquer the impatient strong.

JOHN RUSKIN

Only those who have the patience
to do simple things perfectly
will acquire the skill
to do difficult things easily.

JOHANN SCHILLER

Patience: A minor form of despair,
disguised as a virtue.

AMBROSE BIERCE

Patience and time
do more than strength or passion.

JEAN DE LA FONTAINE

⟶✦⟵

Patience is a necessary ingredient of genius.

BENJAMIN DISRAELI

⟶✦⟵

Patience is bitter,
but its fruits are sweet.

JEAN-JACQUES ROUSSEAU

⟶✦⟵

Patience is passion tamed.

LYMAN ABBOTT

⟶✦⟵

Patience is the companion of wisdom.

ST. AUGUSTINE

Successful salesmen, authors, executives
and workmen of every sort need patience.
The great liability of youth
is not inexperience but impatience.

WILLIAM FEATHER

Possess your soul with patience.

JOHN DRYDEN

The road to success is not to be run upon
by seven-leagued boots.
Step by step, little by little, bit by bit—
that is the way to wealth,
that is the way to wisdom,
that is the way to glory.

CHARLES BUXTON

Success consists of a series of little daily victories.

LADDIE F. HUTAR

There's no music in "rest,"
but there's the making of music in it.
And people are always missing
that part of the life melody,
always talking of perseverance
and courage and fortitude,
but patience is the finest and worthiest part
of fortitude, and the rarest, too.

JOHN RUSKIN

Walking on water wasn't built in a day.

JACK KEROUAC

PERSISTENCE

Vacillating people seldom succeed.
They seldom win the solid respect of their fellows.
Successful men and women are very careful
in reaching decisions and very persistent
and determined in action thereafter.

L. G. ELLIOTT

I find in life that most affairs
that require serious handling are distasteful.
For this reason, I have always believed
that the successful man has the hardest battle
with himself rather than with the other fellow.
To bring one's self to a frame of mind
and to the proper energy to accomplish things
that require plain hard work continuously
is the one big battle that everyone has.
When this battle is won for all time,
then everything is easy.

THOMAS A. BUCKNER

The secret of success
is the consistency to pursue.

HARRY F. BANKS

It is not enough to begin;
continuance is necessary.
Mere enrollment will not make one a scholar;
the pupil must continue in the school
through the long course,
until he masters every branch.
Success depends upon staying power.
The reason for failure in most cases
is lack of perseverance.

J. R. MILLER

Press on. Nothing in the world
can take the place of persistence.

RAY A. KROC

Men who have attained things worth having
in this world have worked while others idled,
have persevered when others gave up in despair,
have practiced early in life
the valuable habits of self-denial, industry,
and singleness of purpose.
As a result, they enjoy in later life
the success so often erroneously attributed
to good luck.

GRENVILLE KLEISER

The great highroad of human welfare
lies along the old highway of steadfast well-doing;
and they who are the most persistent,
and work in the true spirit,
will invariably be the most successful.
Success treads on the heels of every right effort.

SAMUEL SMILES

The man with the average mentality,
but with control, with a definite goal,
and a clear conception of how it can be gained,
and above all, with the power of application
and labor, wins in the end.

WILLIAM HOWARD TAFT

Walter B. Pitkin has written a book on
"Life Begins at Forty." I rise to offer a substitute,
Mr. Pitkin, "Life Begins Each Morning."
Whether one is twenty, forty or sixty;
whether one has succeeded,
failed or just muddled along;
whether yesterday was full of sun or storm,
or one of those dull days with no weather at all,
Life Beings Each Morning! . . .
Each night of life is a wall between today and the past.
Each morning is the open door to a new world—
new vistas, new aims, new tryings.

LEIGH MITCHELL HODGES

All the performances of human art,
at which we look with praise or wonder,
are instances of the resistless force of perseverance.

SAMUEL JOHNSON

The young man who would succeed
must identify his interests with those of his employer
and exercise the same diligence in matters entrusted
to him as he would in his own affairs.
Back of all the gifts a candidate for success may
possess must be a willing capacity for hard work. . . .
Youth today is not considered a handicap
in selecting men for responsible jobs, as it was twenty
years ago. . . . In almost any field today in which a
youngster has an intelligent interest,
the road to the top is open as it never was before.
But the one way to the top
is by persistent, intelligent, hard work.

A. T. MERCIER

TALENT

As tools become rusty, so does the mind;
a garden uncared for
soon becomes smothered in weeds;
a talent neglected withers and dies.

ETHEL R. PAGE

Each man has his own vocation.
The talent is the call.

RALPH WALDO EMERSON

If a man has talent and cannot use it,
he has failed.
If he has a talent and uses only half of it,
he has partly failed.
If he has talent and learns somehow
to use the whole of it, he has gloriously succeeded,
and won a satisfaction and a triumph
few men will ever know.

THOMAS WOLFE

Every natural power exhilarates;
a true talent delights the possessor first.

RALPH WALDO EMERSON

Have success and there will always be fools
to say that you have talent.

EDOUARD PAILLERON

Hidden talent counts for nothing.

NERO

If I have talent and intelligence,
I shall get on;
if not, it isn't worth pulling me out of the mud.

MODEST PETROVICH MUSSORGSKY

In my mind, talent plus knowledge,
plus effort account for success.

GERTRUDE SAMUELS

One well-cultivated talent, deepened and enlarged,
is worth 100 shallow faculties.
The first law of success in this day,
when so many things are clamoring for attention,
is concentration—
to bend all the energies to one point,
and to go directly to that point,
looking neither to the right nor to the left.

WILLIAM MATTHEWS

Not because of an extraordinary talent
did he succeed,
but because he had a capacity
of a level for business and not above it.

TACITUS

One of the greatest talents of all
is the talent to recognize and to develop talent
in others.

FRANK TYGER

Shun no toil
to make yourself remarkable
by some one talent.
Yet do not devote yourself
to one branch exclusively.
Give up no science entirely,
for all science is one.

SENECA

Talent for talent's sake is a bauble and a show.
Talent working with joy in the cause
of universal truth lifts the possessor
to new power as a benefactor.

RALPH WALDO EMERSON

Talent is that which is in a man's power;
genius is that in whose power a man is.

JAMES RUSSELL LOWELL

———

The talent of success is nothing more
than doing what you can do well
and doing well whatever you do
without thought of fame.

HENRY WADSWORTH LONGFELLOW

———

The toughest thing about success
is that you've got to keep on being a success.
Talent is only a starting point in business.
You've got to keep working that talent.

IRVING BERLIN

Wealth

As we look at the oppressed lands
we are forced to the conclusion
that many of the evils which confront them,
and indeed us, today derive directly
from man's service to Mammon.
The creation of godless ideals,
the setting up of wealth, power
and personal success as the chief aims of life,
has contributed more than any other single factor
to precipitate the moral and economic crisis
with which these lands are faced today
and which at present is even overshadowing
and threatening the demoralization
of our own country.

WILLIAM T. GREEN, D.D.

———✦———

Get place and wealth, if possible with grace;
if not, by any means get wealth and place.

ALEXANDER POPE

Wealth may be an excellent thing,
for it means power, leisure and liberty.

JAMES RUSSELL LOWELL

I have no complex about wealth.
I have worked hard for my money,
producing things people need.
I believe that the able industrial leader
who creates wealth and employment
is more worthy of historical notice
than politicians or soldiers.

J. PAUL GETTY

If we fasten our attention on what we have,
rather than on what we lack,
a very little wealth is sufficient.

FRANCIS JOHNSON

Money is an important success symbol
in our culture. Successful people
surround themselves with success symbols—
positive, pragmatic, and supportive examples
of solid accomplishment.

WHITT N. SCHULTZ

⋯⋯

Money may be the husk of many things,
but not the kernel.
It brings you food, but not appetite;
medicine, but not health;
acquaintance, but not friends;
servants, but not loyalty;
days of joy, but not peace or happiness.

HENRIK IBSEN

⋯⋯

High descent and meritorious deeds,
unless united to wealth, are as useless as seaweed.

HORACE

Surplus wealth is a sacred trust
which its possessor is bound to administer
in his lifetime
for the good of the community.

ANDREW CARNEGIE

The ascending spiral of greatness in America
has risen because industry has produced wealth,
which in turn has supported educational institutions,
which in turn have supplied leadership to industry
in order that with each succeeding generation
it might produce more wealth.

WALLACE F. BENNETT

The gratification of wealth
is not found in mere possession
or in lavish expenditure,
but in its wise application.

MIGUEL DE CERVANTES

The old thought that one cannot be rich
except at the expense of his neighbor, must pass away.
True prosperity adds to the richness
of the whole world, such as that of the man
who makes two trees grow
where only one grew before.
The parasitical belief in prosperity
as coming by the sacrifices of others
has no place in the mind that thinks true.
"My benefit is your benefit,
your success is my success,"
should be the basis of all our wealth.

ANNE RIX MILTZ

Wealth is a means to an end, not the end itself.
As a synonym for health and happiness,
it has had a fair trial and failed dismally.

JOHN GALSWORTHY

———

The way to wealth is as plain
as the way to market.
It depends chiefly on two words,
industry and frugality;
that is, waste neither time nor money,
but make the best use of both.
Without industry and frugality nothing will do;
with them, everything.

BENJAMIN FRANKLIN

———

Wealth is not in making money,
but in making the man while he is making money.
Production, not destruction, leads to success.

JOHN WICKER

Traffic is the lifestream of the 20th century.
It is the sign of success and prosperity.
After all, what is a pedestrian?
He is a man who has two cars—
one being driven by his wife,
the other by one of his children.

ROBERT BRADBURY

WISDOM

A man begins cutting his wisdom teeth
the first time he bites off more than he can chew.

HERB CAEN

Keep the gold and keep the silver,
but give us wisdom.

ARABIAN PROVERB

Wisdom is knowing what to do next,
virtue is doing it.

DAVID STARR JORDAN

A prudent person profits from personal experience,
a wise one from the experience of others.

JOSEPH COLLINS

Heads are wisest when they are cool
and hearts are strongest
when they beat in response to noble ideals.

RALPH J. BUNCHE

Be wiser than other people if you can;
but do not tell them so.

PHILIP DORMER STANHOPE,

LORD CHESTERFIELD

It may serve as a comfort to us,
in all our calamities and afflictions,
that he that loses anything and gets wisdom by it
is a gainer by the loss.

ROGER L'ESTRANGE

Having harvested all the knowledge
and wisdom we can from our mistakes and failures,
we should put them behind us and go ahead,
for vain regretting interferes with the flow
of power into our own personalities.

EDITH JOHNSON

———

I have always observed that to succeed in the world
one should appear like a fool but be wise.

MONTESQUIEU

(CHARLES-LOUIS DE SECONDAT)

———

My desire is for wisdom,
not for the exercise of the will.
The will is the strong blind man
who carries on his shoulders
the lame man who can see.

ARTHUR SCHOPENHAUER

Perhaps wisdom is to be found in people
who have suffered greatly but have surmounted it.

LOUIS JOLYON WEST

Success makes a fool seem wise.

H. G. BOHN

The man who makes everything
that leads to happiness depend upon himself,
and not upon other men,
has adopted the very best plan
for living happily.
This is the man of moderation,
the man of manly character and of wisdom.

PLATO

Along with success comes a reputation for wisdom.

EURIPIDES

The road of excess leads to the palace of wisdom;
for we never know what is enough
until we know what is more than enough.

WILLIAM BLAKE

The sum of wisdom
is that time is never lost that is devoted to work.

RALPH WALDO EMERSON

To make no mistakes is not in the power of man;
but from their errors and mistakes
the wise and good learn wisdom for the future.

PLUTARCH

True wisdom is to know
what is best worth knowing,
and to do what is best worth doing.

EDWARD PORTER HUMPHREY

Wisdom and beauty are the twin arches
of that invisible bridge which leads
from the individual conscience—
ever rebellious against its destiny—
to man's collective conscience,
every in search of general progress.

JAIME TORRES BODET

Wisdom consists in rising superior
both to madness and to common sense,
and in lending oneself to the universal illusion
without becoming its dupe.

HENRI FRÉDÉRIC AMIEL

Wisdom denotes the pursuing
of the best ends by the best means.

FRANCES HUTCHESON

Wisdom does not show itself so much in precept
as in life—in firmness of mind
and a mastery of appetite.
It teaches us to do as well as to talk;
and to make our words and actions all of a color.

SENECA

Wisdom is oftimes nearer
when we stoop than when we soar.

WILLIAM WORDSWORTH

INDEX